HAWAI'I'S 2ND

SPAM™

COOKBOOK

Written and Illustrated by
ANN KONDO CORUM

3565 Harding Ave. Honolulu, Hawai'i 96816
808/734-7159   www.besspress.com

Design: Carol Colbath

Library of Congress Cataloging-in-Publication Data

Corum, Ann Kondo.
    Hawai'i's 2nd SPAM™ cookbook /
Ann Kondo Corum.
        p.   cm.
    Includes illustrations, glossary.
    ISBN 1-57306-136-0 hardcover
    ISBN 1-57306-135-2 paperback
    1.   Cookery, Hawaiian.
2. Spam (Trademark). I. Title.
TX724.5.H3C68 2001 641.59969-dc20

With much aloha to all SPAM™ fans. Stand by your SPAM®!

In the land of SPAM®
We love our rice,
Pickle-onion, and rainbow shave ice.
Fried mun doo, kakimochi too,
And two-finger poi like
Thick, sticky glue.

We love teri chicken,
Kal-bi and
Baked ham,
But our favorite meat is
That pink block of SPAM®.

Contents

SPAM is a registered trademark of Hormel Foods, LLC for luncheon meat.

SPAM is a registered trademark of Hormel Foods, LLC for luncheon meat.

SPAM is a registered trademark of Hormel Foods, LLC for luncheon meat.

Preface

There is something about SPAM® luncheon meat that evokes powerful emotions. In Hawai'i it has risen to the status of a cultural icon. Not only do people in Hawai'i really love the taste of SPAM®; they also hold SPAM® close to their hearts. It is Hawai'i's soul food. SPAM® reinforces our social ties to family and friends. It evokes memories: fun days at the beach, good times on the golf course, standing in line at the market to stock up on hurricane food, and carefree after-school stops at the neighborhood mom 'n' pop store or the local 7-Eleven® to buy a SPAM™ musubi. There is no denying that people in Hawai'i have an emotional attachment to SPAM® luncheon meat.

In 1987, when I wrote *Hawai'i's SPAM™ Cookbook*, Hawai'i residents consumed more SPAM® than any other state, about 4 million cans a year, which comes out to six cans per year per person. Happily, it still holds this record, although Guam now rivals Hawai'i as the number one per capita consumer of SPAM®. But why? Even before all the emotional attachment and elevation to icon status of SPAM®, Hawaiians loved this tender pink meat in a can. It goes well with rice, the carbohydrate of choice in the islands. It also goes well with noodles (second carbo choice). Of course it also tastes good with

"Yikes, that's a lot of fat!"

poi! It mixes well with vegetables. And while it isn't exactly a health food, compared with many fast foods it is surprisingly nutritious. Also, because of the high humidity in Hawai'i, we perspire a lot, and salty SPAM® replaces lost electrolytes (SPAMMAN™—more about him later—says this is true). But the bottom line is, we just like it!

But why another SPAM™ cookbook after all the ribbing and joking I've endured? Because there are more ways to slice a block of SPAM® luncheon meat and have fun with it. This book is also an attempt to record the latest developments in one small segment of local food culture. Hawai'i, with its wonderful ethnic mix and serious attitude toward food, inspires people to try things, including SPAM®, in different ways. Creative cooks have offered me new recipes, including those from SPAM™ cooking contests, such as Honolulu's SPAMARAMA™ and Maui's SPAM™ Cook-Off, which have becomes serious competitions in the islands. SPAM® luncheon meat has risen to heights beyond the SPAM™ musubi (although this is still a favorite). Here you will find a bit of SPAM® in many local-style recipes. Some are blatantly fat-packed (but nobody eats SPAM® every day), many are quick and easy to prepare, and some have ties to our past. A few favorite recipes from the original *Hawai'i's SPAM™ Cookbook* (on pages 28, 68, 102, 117, 124, and 128) have been repeated, but the majority of the recipes are new to this book.

A big mahalo to all the SPAM™ fans who so graciously shared their recipes and thoughts about SPAM® with me. And to all my friends who endured the "SPAM™ Trials," thank you for your testing and tasting and helpful feedback.

Remember, as always, recipes are only guidelines. Substitute ingredients and add your personal touch. Cooking can be fun, and who knows?—you may be the person to elevate SPAM® luncheon meat to a gourmet level without compromising its integrity! I hope this book makes you smile.

Some SPAM™ Notes

As all SPAM® luncheon meat eaters know, there are three types of plain SPAM®: regular, lite, and 25% less sodium. What you use is a personal preference; it doesn't matter which one you use in these recipes, although you may want to cut back on soy sauce or other salty ingredients if you use the regular. I prefer the lite for general recipes, but for SPAM™ musubi, I like 25% less sodium.

Flavored SPAM® is also available, although purists like plain-old SPAM® best. Smoke Flavored SPAM® and now Hot & Spicy SPAM® (available in Hawai'i and Guam) are flavors you might like to try in some of these recipes. Smoke Flavored SPAM® lends itself better to haole-style dishes than to Asian-style dishes. Hot & Spicy SPAM® works well with dishes using fresh veggies or in Mexican-style dishes. Turkey SPAM®, while not really SPAM® flavored, is low in fat and works well in some recipes, such as casseroles.

In many of the recipes, SPAM® is cut into what I call "logs." This is merely a way to nicely mix SPAM® luncheon meat with other ingredients, particularly veggies. To make logs, just slice SPAM® lengthwise, usually 8 slices, then cut those slices crosswise (usually). Some recipes call for logs cut lengthwise.

SPAM® is very easy to grate, mash, or chop. For most recipes calling for ground SPAM®, I use the small holes of a grater.

Unless stated otherwise in the recipes, a can of SPAM® luncheon meat refers to a 12-ounce can.

SPAM® Luncheon Meat for Athletes?

Bob Brubaker, aka the SPAMMAN™, is a triathlete who proudly professes his "healthy devotion" to SPAM® luncheon meat. Yes, Hormel Foods does sponsor him in competitions; however, he ate SPAM® even before the sponsorship. Bob says, "The SPAM® connection is perfect for an endurance athlete. I like the product; yes, I eat the product three or four times per week, and have found success in my training." Athletes who train hard, especially in warm, humid climates, get depleted in electrolytes, and the salt in SPAM® is a benefit. Also, when one works out as hard as the SPAMMAN™, a little fat is beneficial. The SPAMMAN™ has participated in events in Hawai'i and says, "The people of Hawai'i show so much love for SPAM® luncheon meat and the SPAMMAN™ that I feel like I really represent them, along with SPAM® lovers everywhere."

Included in this book are two recipes shared with aloha by the SPAMMAN™. These dishes, created by his wife, Jan (aka SPAMM'AM™), are Power Balls (page 37) and SPAMMAN™ Casserole (page 44). Those sound like powerful foods, don't they?

SPAMARAMA™

There are other SPAMARAMA™ festivals around the country, but the Honolulu SPAMA-RAMA™, begun only a couple of years ago by Dawn Isa, probably has a wider and richer assortment of entries than any other because of the multiethnic makeup of the city and the various backgrounds of the participants. Also, because of the aloha Hawai'i residents have for SPAM® luncheon meat, the recipes reflect this spirit. Dave Mozdren, whose fat-packed winning recipe for SPAM™-Apple Quiche is on page 100, became a SPAM® convert only after he moved to the islands from the mainland. That's what moving to Hawai'i does to you!

More SPAM™ Facts

For more information and trivia on SPAM® luncheon meat than you ever imagined possible, I refer you to *SPAM®: A Biography*, by Carolyn Wyman (Harcourt, Brace and Company, 1999), a truly comprehensive book covering all aspects of SPAM®. Lots of fun to read.

Aunty Momona's Predictions for the Future of SPAM® Luncheon Meat

- Zero-calorie SPAM® luncheon meat will be developed, and it will taste as good and greasy-salty as ever.
- The SPAM™ Diet will be the new training diet for triathletes.
- Celebrity chefs will fuse SPAM® and Euro-Asian and Mexican cooking with Pacific Rim cuisine to create the ultimate dining experience in Hawai'i.
- The Tropic of SPAM™, running through the Hawaiian Islands, will be created and all maps and globes will have to be reconfigured.
- Travelers flying between Hawai'i and the Mainland will be able to request SPAM™ musubi, but only if they call ahead.
- Transplanted Hawaiians will be able to download SPAM™ musubi from the Internet.

"And here we are at the Tropic of SPAM™."

5

SPAM™ Musubi (moo-sue-bee)

Of all the ways Hawaiians eat SPAM® luncheon meat, SPAM™ musubi is definitely the most popular. It's easy to see why it is Hawai'i's favorite fast food. Everybody has a favorite way of making SPAM™ musubi. Some people prefer the SPAM® plain, while others like it seasoned. Some musubi are made sandwich-style, with the slice of SPAM® between two layers of rice. Honolulu City Councilman and former National Motocross Champion John DeSoto fondly remembers his family calling this SPAM® and rice concoction "DeSPAM™wich"—local-style sandwich. Indeed, like a sandwich, musubi includes the satisfying combination of protein and carbohydrates in a portable package.

Besides being portable and convenient, musubi is very satisfying to eat. It is local comfort food. Many locals who are now living elsewhere admit that one of the things they miss about Hawai'i is SPAM™ musubi. And after traveling in Europe and eating gourmet food for weeks, I must admit the thing I wanted most to eat upon returning to Hawai'i was SPAM™ musubi!

Parents stop at little mom 'n' pop stores so that kids can buy a musubi for breakfast or a snack, golfers buy it on the golf course, and it is available everywhere from Longs Drugs to 7-Eleven® stores for anyone who wants a quick bite to eat. While SPAM™ musubi has been called junk food, it is no worse than a hot dog or a slice of cheese and pepperoni pizza, especially if it is made with Lite SPAM® luncheon meat. (See nutritional analysis of SPAM™ musubi at the end of this section. For comparison and analysis of other foods see USDA Nutrient Data Lab website:www.nal.usda.gov/fnic/foodcomp.)

When did the SPAM™ musubi make its appearance in Hawai'i? Nobody is able to pin-point its exact birth date, but guesses range from the 1960s to the 1970s. Perhaps Mrs. Mitsuko Kaneshiro was one of the first people making SPAM™ musubi commercially. She remembers making SPAM®, Vienna sausage, and hot dog musubi for her children's snack in 1963. Her first commercial venture was selling SPAM™ musubi at the old City Pharmacy on Pensacola Street (one dozen SPAM™musubi that disappeared in five min-utes). Later, she sold musubi to blind vendors to resell at their stands in the municipal building, the old downtown post office, the old police station, circuit court building, and other office buildings in downtown Honolulu. At the peak of her musubi career in the early 1980s, Mrs. Kaneshiro made musubi at her shop, Michan's Musubi, on the corner of King and Houghtailing streets, delivering almost 500 musubi per day, using her son Ted as the delivery boy. Mrs. Kaneshiro's musubi were made individually, without a musubi maker. Sandy Pak, a former teacher, remembers her first SPAM™ musubi as an oval-shaped mom-made treat from her student Mitzi Kaneshiro. Today, there are com-mercial contraptions that can turn out 500 musubi at a time, and thousands of musubi are sold commercially throughout Hawai'i.

This hybrid of the standard Japanese musubi (riceball) is now uniquely part of our local food legacy and we love it! When I wrote *Hawai'i's SPAM™ Cookbook* in 1987, I included SPAM™ musubi; however, at that time the acrylic SPAM™ musubi maker was not prevalent. SPAM™ musubi in those days were more oval-shaped because they were formed by hand. Some people packed the rice in the empty SPAM® luncheon meat can

"Eh, Tiger, do we come here to play golf or eat SPAM™ musubi?"

to achieve a nice, uniform shape. Now, with the use of the musubi maker, an acrylic box with no top or bottom and a "pusher" to pack the rice, its shape is a neat rectangle with corners.

Did you know that SPAM™ musubi can be frozen? Wrap them well in plastic wrap and store in freezer bags. They are so handy to have for a snack or for lunch at work; just pop one into the microwave and heat and eat. And to make SPAM™ musubi for a crowd, pat your rice into a large baking pan, lay SPAM® luncheon meat slices on top, cut through the rice at the SPAM® "markers," and then wrap each bundle in nori.

SPAM™ Musubi Platter

For your next get-together, why not do a SPAM™ musubi platter instead of a sushi platter? Here are some suggestions.

The Classic

Everybody loves the plain-old SPAM™ musubi. For those of you who do not live in Hawai'i, here is the way to make the classic SPAM™ musubi.

Slice SPAM® luncheon meat into 8 pieces (if you're real cheap, 10 slices), lengthwise.

Cook rice. An average musubi will take about 1 cup cooked rice. It is important to use medium-grain rice, such as Calrose, and not instant rice.

Fry SPAM®. Some like it barely browned, while others like it almost crunchy. It's all a matter of taste.

Almost everyone in Hawai'i has a SPAM™ musubi maker, which forms rice into a nice, neat SPAM™ shape, but if you don't, just shape rice by hand into the shape of a skinny SPAM™ can.

Cut nori (seaweed sheets) in half. (Again, if you're cheap, you can make more pieces.) Lay nori on a piece of plastic wrap with the narrow end facing you. Put the dampened musubi maker on the center of the nori. Put some rice in it, press rice down with press, and then place SPAM® luncheon meat on top. Some people like plenty of rice and others prefer less rice, so adjust rice-SPAM® ratio according to taste. Sometimes I put ume (pickled plum) in the middle of the rice layer. Roll nori around SPAM® and rice, and wrap musubi in plastic wrap.

Sato-Shoyu (Sugar-Soy) SPAM™ Musubi

Just like the classic, except cook SPAM® luncheon meat slices for a few minutes in mixture of equal parts soy sauce and sugar with a little water added (or use bottled teriyaki sauce). Drain and place on rice; roll nori around rice and SPAM®.

The Deluxe

Make a Japanese omelet by mixing together the following: 3 eggs, 1 teaspoon water, 1 teaspoon soy sauce, $1/2$ teaspoon sugar, and pinch of salt. Heat a little oil in skillet or omelet pan. Pour in eggs, cook until set on low heat and then flip or roll eggs. Flip eggs out of pan and cut into slices (so they fit on musubi). Make and form rice as you would for classic SPAM™ musubi. Sprinkle furikake nori (seasoned, flaked seaweed) or tsukudani nori (wet nori in a jar) on rice before putting egg and SPAM® on it. Roll nori around musubi.

Green Eggs and SPAM™ Musubi

Follow directions above, except tint eggs green before cooking them and add some chopped green onion. You can also add a thin layer of wasabi (Japanese horseradish) on rice for an additional touch of green.

Green Rice and SPAM™ Musubi

Add a few drops of green food coloring to water before cooking rice for musubi. (Good for St. Patrick's Day or UH tailgate party.) The lovely pink meat, green rice, and black nori make an eye-popping combination. To add a little red to the bundle, you can place some shredded pickled Japanese ginger (bright-red kind) or ume (pickled plum) on rice. Cut musubi in half so layers of color can be appreciated.

The Korean

Before forming your rice, put it in large bowl and add 2 teaspoons sesame seeds and 1–2 tablespoons sesame oil (to approximately 3 cups cooked rice). Mix well, make musubi, and place some drained and finely chopped won bok kim chee (Korean pickled cabbage) on rice before putting SPAM® luncheon meat on it. Roll nori around bundle.

Fried Rice SPAM™ Musubi

Prepare fried rice (p. 68, or according to your favorite recipe). When using fried rice you will have to pack it down, as it tends to be drier than basic steamed rice. Place SPAM® luncheon meat on top and roll nori around it.

The Veggie

Put thin layer of mayonnaise on musubi. Slice cucumbers very thinly and arrange on mayo. Place SPAM® luncheon meat on top of cucumbers and add some finely shredded lettuce. Roll nori around it. Sometimes this one can get bambucha (very big) so you may have to use a bigger piece of nori to wrap it.

Kona Coffee Musubi

This musubi created by Corin Kelly and Caroline Orita was a first-place winner in the Kona Coffee Festival recipe contest. The SPAM® luncheon meat slices take on a subtle coffee flavor.

    Heat until sugar dissolves: 2 cups strong Kona coffee, 1 cup soy sauce, and 1 cup sugar. Marinate SPAM® slices in mixture overnight. Pan-fry SPAM® slices. Place on rice and roll nori around it. Serve at once.

"SPAM" is in the mind of the beholder.

Sesame-Crusted Musubi

This is one instance in which nori is not used to hold the bundle together.

Prepare SPAM® luncheon meat slices to taste (fried or sato-shoyu). Put layer of rice in musubi maker (not too thick), then SPAM® slice, and more rice. Press down on top layer firmly. Wrap thin strip of nori around it. Place roasted sesame seeds on piece of waxed paper and roll musubi in them. Heat about 1 teaspoon of oil in nonstick skillet and brown musubi on both sides. Cut musubi in thirds to make it easier to eat. The roasted sesame seeds add crunch and a delicious aroma! This musubi is not as portable as ones wrapped in more nori, but it makes a different addition to musubi platters.

Koko Musubi

Prepare rice and fry SPAM® luncheon meat. Form rice as you would for classic SPAM® musubi. Spread a thin layer of tsukudani nori on the rice along with layers of thinly sliced takuwan and/or sambaizuke (Japanese pickled veggies). Top with SPAM® luncheon meat and roll nori around musubi.

SPAM™usushi

If you want to get fancy, try making sushi with SPAM® luncheon meat. You will need cooked rice, fried SPAM® cut into logs, tsukudani nori or ume (pickled plums), and sheets of sushi nori.

For each SPAM™usushi, lay piece of nori on bamboo sushi roller or piece of waxed paper (or use plastic sushi mold). Place layer of rice on sheet of nori, leaving about 1 inch bare on one length (opposite your body). Spread some nori or ume down middle. Lay SPAM™ logs on top and roll up. For variety you can add ingredients such as cucumber strips, drained and chopped kim chee, takuwan, ume, or fried egg strips to SPAM®. Try different combinations, such as hot-dog mustard and dill pickle strips or mayo, cucumber strips, and avocado. Slice like sushi.

Nutritional Analysis of SPAM™ Musubi
(courtesy of the *Honolulu Advertiser* Food Section)

The analysis is based on a 1.3-ounce slice of regular SPAM® luncheon meat (equivalent to a slice from a one-can block sliced into 9 pieces), 1 cup medium-grain rice, such as Calrose, and a strip of nori.

SPAM® contains 113 calories and 10.6 grams of fat.

A cup of rice contains 266 calories, 0.4 grams of protein, 58.6 grams of carbohydrates, and some minerals.

Nori has 35 calories in 3.5 ounces and 0.3 grams of fat. It is also a source of vitamin A, calcium, and traces of other vitamins and minerals. However, only a strip of nori is used in musubi.

Considering these ingredients, a SPAM™ musubi probably has just under 400 calories, about 11 grams of fat, and 9.5 grams of protein.

Pūpū

In December of 1987, after *Hawai'i's SPAM™ Cookbook* was published, I received "fan mail" from a young man who wanted to share some recipes that I left out. I saved that letter because it was full of humor as well as good ideas, not even thinking there would ever be a *Hawai'i's 2nd SPAM™ Cookbook*! There was no return address on the envelope, now yellowed with age, and all I knew was that this guy was a Kam School grad. Through the wonders of the World Wide Web, I was able to locate Robert G. (Bobby) Hill III of Maui, now a grown-up police sergeant, who fears that his salad-eating colleagues will excommunicate him from nutrition circles because of his affiliation with SPAM® luncheon meat. The truth always comes out, Bobby! Thank you for sharing your recipes.

Bobby's SPAM™-Shimi

Delicately filet SPAM® luncheon meat and place decoratively on chopped cabbage. Serve with hot mustard or ketchup. Serve after REAL sashimi runs out and guests are drunk. Wooden chopsticks suggested.

Hurricane pūpū?

"Since 'ahi was thirty dollars a pound, I have a special treat for you—SPAM™-Shimi!"

Valley Isle Fried Tofu and SPAM™ Appetizer

Serves 6

1 can SPAM® luncheon meat, finely diced
$^1/_2$ cup fishcake ('ō'io or surimi)
$^1/_2$ cup chopped Maui onion
1 tablespoon minced ginger
1 teaspoon pepper
1 tablespoon sesame oil
5 pieces shiitake mushroom, soaked in 1 cup water
1 (14-ounce) can chicken broth
1 tablespoon oyster sauce
1 dozen squares fried tofu (aburage)

Place diced SPAM® in mixing bowl; add fishcake, onion, ginger, pepper, and sesame oil. Squeeze water out of mushrooms and chop them fine. Save mushroom water for broth. Cut fried tofu in halves and parboil in large pot for 3 minutes. Squeeze and drain well.

Stuff each piece of fried tofu with 1–2 tablespoons of SPAM™ mixture.

In large pan, combine chicken broth, oyster sauce, and shiitake mushroom broth.

Add stuffed tofu SPAM™-side-down in pan and simmer for about 20 minutes or until most of broth is gone. Place appetizers SPAM™-side-up on platter and garnish with cilantro.

Note: If fishcake is not available where you live, substitute shrimp that has been processed in food processor.

This first-prize winner from Maui (Wailuku Natsu Matsuri SPAM™ recipe contest) was developed by Anna Mayeda, whose family runs the Valley Isle Tofu Factory.

SPAM is a registered trademark of Hormel Foods, LLC for luncheon meat.

25

SPAM® and Bean Sprouts

Serves 4

1 (10-ounce) package bean sprouts
$^1/_2$ can SPAM® luncheon meat, cut into logs
1 teaspoon toasted sesame seeds
2 tablespoons soy sauce
2 tablespoons vinegar
1 tablespoon vegetable oil
1 tablespoon sesame oil

In large pot, boil water and pinch of salt. Blanch bean sprouts and drain. Rinse with cold water. Brown SPAM® in skillet. Smash sesame seeds with back of large knife or spoon. Mix seeds together with soy, vinegar, and oils. Toss together SPAM®, bean sprouts, and dressing just before serving.

Easy Cheesy SPAM™ Crisps

Serves 8–10

1 (8-ounce) package cream cheese, softened
2 tablespoons mayonnaise
2 teaspoons Worcestershire sauce
2 stalks green onion, minced
won ton wrappers
1 can SPAM® luncheon meat, cut into logs
vegetable oil for frying

Combine cream cheese, mayonnaise, Worcestershire sauce, and green onion in small bowl. Spread about 1 teaspoon of cream cheese mixture in middle of won ton wrapper. Place SPAM® log on top of cream cheese. Moisten edges of wrapper with water and fold in half into rectangle. Press edges together. Deep-fry in oil heated to 350 degrees until golden. Drain on paper towels.

SPAM™ Won Ton

Serves 6–8

1 can SPAM® luncheon meat, grated or finely minced
1/2 cup water chestnuts, chopped
2 stalks green onion, sliced
1/2 teaspoon pepper
1 tablespoon oyster sauce

1 egg
1 tablespoon cornstarch
1 teaspoon sugar
1 package won ton wrappers
vegetable oil for frying

Mix all ingredients together (except wrappers and oil). Place generous teaspoon of mixture on wrapper, form triangle, and seal edges. Deep-fry in oil heated to 350 degrees until won ton is golden brown. Drain on paper towels. Serve with mustard-shoyu.

Mustard-shoyu:
1 tablespoon dry mustard
1 tablespoon cold water
2–3 tablespoons soy sauce

Mix all ingredients until smooth, adding more soy sauce if necessary.

How to wrap won ton

Empanadas de SPAM™

Serves 10

1 potato, coarsely grated
vegetable oil
1 can SPAM® luncheon meat, grated (or use Hot & Spicy SPAM® and omit jalapeño pepper)
$1/2$ cup onion, minced
1 teaspoon cumin
1 jalapeño pepper, seeded and chopped
1 tomato, diced
$1/2$ cup grated Jack cheese
$1/4$ cup chopped cilantro
mun doo or gyoza wrappers

Grate potato and put in cold water until ready to use; drain well before using. Heat a little oil in skillet and cook together SPAM®, onion, potato, cumin, jalapeño pepper, and tomato until potato is tender. Cool and mix in cheese and cilantro. Place teaspoonful of SPAM™ mixture on each mun doo wrapper. Moisten edges and seal with fork. Deep-fry in hot oil until golden brown. Serve with prepared salsa.

SPAM™-Maki

Serves 6

$1/2$ can SPAM® luncheon meat, cut into logs
1 pound fishcake ('ō'io or surimi)
2 stalks green onion, finely chopped
1 carrot, grated
6 water chestnuts, finely chopped

1 tablespoon sugar
$1/2$ teaspoon pepper
5–6 sheets nori, cut in half
vegetable oil for frying
waxed paper or plastic wrap

Cut SPAM® and set aside. Mix together all ingredients except nori and oil. Place nori on piece of waxed paper. Spread fishcake mixture on piece of nori, leaving $3/4$-inch margin with no filling along top and bottom of nori. Place SPAM™ log in middle and roll up like sushi. Wrap roll in waxed paper or plastic wrap, place in freezer bag, and freeze overnight or longer. Slice each roll into 4 pieces while still frozen. Fry in oil heated to 350 degrees until lightly browned. Serve with wasabi-soy or mustard-soy sauce.

Note: If you live where there is no prepared fishcake, substitute shrimp that has been processed in food processor.

Stuffed Aburage

Serves 4-6

8 pieces aburage (fried tofu)
boiling water
1 cup water
$^1/_4$ cup soy sauce
3 tablespoons sugar
pinch of salt
cornstarch

$^1/_2$ can SPAM® luncheon meat, finely grated
2 stalks green onion, finely chopped
1 $^1/_2$ tablespoons sake
1 tablespoon soy sauce
2 teaspoons sesame seeds
1 egg
$^1/_4$ cup prepared breadcrumbs

Place aburage pieces in bowl, pour boiling water over them, and drain. Cut aburage in half so you have 16 pieces. In pan, heat water, $^1/_4$ cup soy, sugar, and salt. Cook aburage in sauce for about 5 minutes. Drain on paper towels.

Mix together SPAM®, green onion, sake, 1 tablespoon soy, sesame seeds, egg, and breadcrumbs.

Lay seasoned aburage on waxed paper and sprinkle with cornstarch. Spread SPAM™ mixture on each aburage. Do not spread filling completely to edge. Roll as you would sushi and fasten with toothpicks. Steam 20 minutes. Remove toothpicks and cut into slices.

Serve with wasabi mixed with soy sauce.

SPAM™ Summer Rolls

bahn trang (rice-paper rounds)
SPAM® luncheon meat logs
somen noodles, cooked according to directions
leaf lettuce
finely slivered cucumber
finely slivered carrots
mint
cilantro

Arrange SPAM® and other ingredients on large platter or tray. Provide shallow dish of warm water for dipping bahn trang to soften. Each person makes his own roll by placing ingredients in softened wrapper. Do not overstuff. Serve with dipping sauce.

Peanut Dipping Sauce
$1/2$ cup hoi sin sauce
$1/4$ cup water
2 tablespoons peanut butter
1 teaspoon minced garlic
1–2 teaspoons hot sauce (chili paste or Tabasco®)
2 tablespoons finely chopped peanuts

SPAM™mies

Serves 4

1 can SPAM® luncheon meat (lite or 25% less sodium), mashed fine
1 large potato, boiled and mashed
$1/_2$ cup imitation crab, cut into pieces and shredded
$1/_2$ cup finely chopped onion
1 tablespoon sugar
pinch of garlic powder
dash of pepper
2 tablespoons mochiko (rice flour)
1 tablespoon furikake nori
1 egg
vegetable oil for frying

Combine and mix SPAM®, potato, crab, onion, sugar, garlic powder, and pepper. Mix in egg, mochiko, and furikake. Mix well. Form into small balls and flatten to make SPAM™mies. Fry in about 1 tablespoon oil until brown.

SPAM™mies, by Kellen Yap of Haiku, won a prize at the Wailuku town Natsu Matsuri SPAM™ recipe contest. Note: If you live where mochiko is not available, substitute flour or cornstarch.

Tropical SPAM®

Serves 6–8

1 can SPAM® luncheon meat, finely diced (or use Hot & Spicy SPAM® and omit chili pepper)
1 tomato, diced
1 small Maui onion, chopped
1 mango, diced
1 cup fresh pineapple, diced
$1/4$ cup chopped cilantro
1 Hawaiian chili pepper (or jalapeño) chopped
2 tablespoons lime juice
1 tablespoon soy sauce

Mix all ingredients together. Serve with large tortilla or taro chips.

Power Balls
(a SPAMMAN™ favorite)

Serves 6

1 small onion, finely chopped
$1/2$ can SPAM® luncheon meat, finely chopped
6 tablespoons butter
1 (10-ounce) package frozen chopped spinach
1 cup cornbread stuffing mix
$1/2$ cup finely grated Swiss cheese
2 eggs
$1/4$ teaspoon nutmeg

Sauté onion and SPAM® in butter. Add frozen spinach that has been squeezed dry. Combine SPAM™-spinach mixture with remaining ingredients in food processor. (Or mix well in bowl.)

Shape into 1-inch balls and bake on an ungreased sheet pan in a 350-degree oven until heated through (about 15 minutes).

Serve with sauce made out of $1/2$ cup mayo and 1 tablespoon horseradish.

Note: Power Balls may be frozen on baking sheet and stored in freezer bag after they harden. Bake frozen balls for 20–25 minutes at 350 degrees when needed.

A recipe from Jan Brubaker, wife of SPAMMAN™.

Taro Balls

Serves 10–12

4 cups mashed taro
3 tablespoons panko or flour
$1/2$ can SPAM® luncheon meat, finely chopped
1 Hawaiian chili pepper, chopped
water
salt to taste
vegetable oil for frying

Cut taro in chunks and cook in water until it can be pierced with fork or chopstick. Drain, peel, and mash. Place in bowl with panko or flour, SPAM®, and chili pepper. Add water slowly to make dough that will hold together. Taste and add salt if necessary. Shape into small balls and fry in oil that has been heated to 350 degrees. Drain on paper towels.

Other ingredients such as chopped green onion, water chestnuts, or chopped shiitake mushrooms may be added.

SPAM™ Spread

Serves 8–10

$1/_2$ can SPAM® luncheon meat, grated
1 (8-ounce) package cream cheese, softened
1 teaspoon grated onion
1 tablespoon lemon juice
2 teaspoons prepared horseradish
2 tablespoons chopped parsley
$1/_2$ cup mango chutney

Combine all ingredients except chutney. With clean hands, form mixture into SPAM™ shape. Spread chutney on top and serve with crackers.

Pinwheels

Serves 8–10

1 (8-ounce) package cream cheese, softened
2 teaspoons chili powder
1 clove minced garlic
Tabasco® sauce to taste (optional)
2 tablespoons chopped cilantro
1 (4-ounce) can chopped green chilies
1 (4-ounce) can sliced olives
$^1/_2$ can SPAM® luncheon meat, grated (or Hot & Spicy SPAM®)
6 10-inch tortillas (flour, whole wheat, or spinach)

In bowl, mix together all ingredients except tortillas. Spread some of mixture on each tortilla and roll up like jellyroll. Wrap rolls in plastic wrap and chill at least 1 hour before slicing. Cut into 1 $^1/_2$-inch pieces and serve with bottled salsa.

Green Eggs and SPAM®

4 servings

8 hard-boiled eggs, peeled and halved
green food coloring
6 tablespoons mayonnaise
2 tablespoons minced green onion
$1/2$ teaspoon dry mustard
salt and pepper to taste
$1/4$–$1/2$ can SPAM® luncheon meat, grated

Spoon yolks from hard-boiled eggs into small bowl. In another bowl, put some water and a few drops of green food coloring. Place whites in this mixture and dye them green. Drain well on paper towels.

Mash egg yolks and add mayonnaise, green onion, and mustard. Spoon yolks into green-tinted whites. Make an indentation in each mound of yolk and spoon in grated SPAM®. Put a bit of remaining grated SPAM® on platter and set green eggs on nest of SPAM®.

I couldn't resist this tribute to Dr. Seuss, one of my favorite author-illustrators!

Main Dishes

good

SPAMMAN™ Casserole

Serves 6–8

1 (10-ounce) package frozen chopped spinach
5 ounces egg noodles
1 can Smoke Flavored SPAM® luncheon meat, diced
1 (15-ounce) can tomato sauce
$1/2$ onion, chopped
garlic salt and pepper to taste

3 tablespoons milk
1 teaspoon sugar
1 (8-ounce) package cream cheese, softened
8 ounces sour cream
1 cup grated Cheddar cheese

Cook and drain frozen spinach. Cook egg noodles and drain.
In large bowl, mix together SPAM®, tomato sauce, onion, and seasonings. Place drained and squeezed spinach in another bowl and mix in milk, sugar, cream cheese, and sour cream. Add spinach mixture to SPAM™ mixture along with cooked noodles. Pour into greased 9x13-inch pan or large casserole dish. Top with grated cheese and bake at 375 degrees for 30–40 minutes.

SPINACH

SPA

This SPAMMAN™ favorite comes from SPAMM'AM™, Jan Brubaker. Recipe too fat-packed? Work out harder!

44

SPAM™-Cabbage-Tomatoes

Serves 6

1 can SPAM® luncheon meat
1 tablespoon oil
1 small onion, sliced
1 medium cabbage, cut into chunks
2 tomatoes, cut into large chunks
1 teaspoon sugar
black pepper to taste

Cut SPAM® into logs. Heat oil in wok or large skillet and lightly brown SPAM®. Add onion and cook for 1 minute. Add cabbage and cook until it is soft, but not mushy. Add tomatoes, sugar, and pepper and cook for 2 minutes. Eat with hot rice.

I was trying to locate a recipe for a SPAM® and tomato dish that was served at Lahaina Bakery years ago. Nobody could recall its ingredients; however, just talking about it inspired a certain Lolly of Lahaina to cook up this concoction. Who knows, it may become the new Lahaina classic! As the guru of good things would say, this dish is VERY excellent.

Local-Style SPAM™ Burritos

Serves 4–6

1 can SPAM® luncheon meat
4 large shiitake mushrooms
$1/2$ Maui onion, thinly sliced
2 carrots, cut into matchstick slivers
2–3 cups finely shredded cabbage or won bok
2 stalks green onion, sliced in 1-inch lengths
$1/2$ teaspoon pepper
1 teaspoon oyster sauce
pinch of red pepper flakes
flour tortillas
hoi sin sauce
cilantro, chopped

Slice SPAM® into 8 pieces, lengthwise, then crosswise into logs. Soak mushrooms in warm water for 15 minutes; squeeze out water and slice into strips.

Heat skillet or wok and coat lightly with cooking spray. Brown SPAM®. Add round onion and carrots and cook about 1 minute. Add shredded cabbage and shiitake mushrooms and cook another minute. Add pepper, oyster sauce, and green onion. Veggies should be crunchy.

To serve: Heat flour tortillas a few seconds in microwave. Spread hoi sin sauce on tortillas and offer filling and chopped cilantro to each person.

Note: If you like your food hot, add chopped Hawaiian chili pepper or jalapeño pepper to filling, or use Hot & Spicy SPAM® luncheon meat.

Aunty Momona rejoices upon reading that Hawai'i will be the test market for the giant economy-size SPAM®.

SPAM® and Potatoes

Serves 4

2 potatoes
1 tablespoon vegetable oil
1 can SPAM® luncheon meat, cut into logs
1 small onion, sliced
1 1/2 teaspoons sugar
black pepper to taste
1/3 cup water
3 stalks green onion, cut into 1-inch pieces

Cut potatoes into strips so they resemble French fries. Parboil in pan of water (about 8 minutes) or microwave until partially cooked. Heat oil in large skillet and brown SPAM®. Add onion and cook 2 minutes. Add water and partially cooked potatoes. Season with sugar and pepper. Cover pan and cook until potatoes are done, adding more water if necessary. Turn off heat and add green onion.

SPAM™ Pinacbet

Serves 4–6

1 tablespoon vegetable oil
1/2 can SPAM® luncheon meat, cut into logs
2 tablespoons minced ginger
2 tablespoons minced garlic
1 round onion, chopped
1 large tomato, cubed
1 tablespoon soy sauce
1/2 cup chicken broth
2 tablespoons bagoong (fish sauce)
black pepper to taste
3 bittermelon, sliced
3 long eggplants, sliced
1/2 pound long beans, cut in 1 1/2-inch pieces
1/4 pound okra
1/2 small kabocha pumpkin, cubed

In large pot, heat oil and lightly brown SPAM®. Add ginger, garlic, onion, and tomato and cook 2 minutes. Add chicken broth and seasonings. Add vegetables and cook until tender, adding more broth or water if necessary.

This is a Filipino-style vegetable stew based on a recipe from Mrs. Garcia (formerly Mrs. Agtarap), who suggested recipes for my first SPAM™ cookbook. If you like more meat, use the whole can of SPAM® luncheon meat. Other vegetables, such as chayote, string beans, or banana squash, may be substituted for the ones listed.

Cabbage Rolls

Serves 4

1 (10-ounce) package frozen chopped spinach
1 can SPAM® luncheon meat, ground or grated (or Turkey SPAM®)
$1/_2$ pound ground turkey (or Turkey SPAM®)
1 small onion, chopped
1 (11-ounce) can tomato soup
1 cup cooked rice (brown or white)
$1/_2$ cup water
2 tablespoons vinegar
1 head cabbage

Thaw spinach and squeeze out water. In large skillet cook together SPAM®, turkey, and onion. Stir in $1/_4$ cup of soup, spinach, and rice. Set aside.

Boil water in large pot. Add whole cabbage and cook until leaves are soft enough to remove. Remove 8 leaves; drain. Spoon SPAM™ mixture onto each leaf and roll up. Fasten with toothpicks. Put back in skillet. Mix together remaining soup, water, and vinegar. Pour over rolls. Cover and cook over low heat 45 minutes.

You may also cook this in the oven (cover pan with foil) for 45 minutes at 350 degrees. One member of the SPAM™ Trials test team forgot the rolls were in her oven and went tidepooling for three hours. When she came home the rolls were well done, but very good!

52

Southwest Kim Chee Pizza

Serves 4

$1/2$ can SPAM® luncheon meat, thinly sliced crosswise (or Hot & Spicy SPAM®)
1 cup prepared salsa
1 16-inch prepared pizza crust
2 cups won bok kim chee, chopped and squeezed
2 cups shredded Mozzarella cheese
powdered kim chee mix, to taste
Parmesan cheese

Preheat oven to 425 degrees. Brown SPAM® slices until almost crispy. Spread salsa over crust. Layer kim chee, SPAM®, and Mozzarella cheese. Sprinkle with kim chee powder and Parmesan cheese. Place on baking sheet and bake for 10–15 minutes.

Other veggies, such as thinly sliced zucchini, bell peppers, and onion, may be added.

Small pizza crusts can be used to make individual-sized pizzas. Good cold.

Thanks to Chris Worrall for being my official Kim Chee Pizza tester!

Maui SPAM™ Croquettes

Serves 4

1 can SPAM® luncheon meat, mashed
1 large potato, boiled and mashed
$1/4$ pound ground pork, browned and drained
$1/2$ Maui onion, chopped
4–5 water chestnuts, chopped
1 small bunch green onions, chopped
salt to taste
oyster sauce to taste
1 egg, beaten
vegetable oil for frying

Mix together all ingredients, except oil. Heat oil in skillet. Form patties and fry them until crisp.

James "Kimo" Apana, Mayor of Maui, contributed this recipe.

54

Curry-Potato SPAM™ Cakes

Serves 6

3 potatoes, boiled and mashed
1 can SPAM® luncheon meat, grated or finely chopped
1 small onion, chopped
1 teaspoon pepper
$1/4$ teaspoon salt
$1/2$ teaspoon sugar

1 tablespoon curry powder
1 egg
flour
2 eggs, beaten
panko or fine breadcrumbs
vegetable oil

Mash cooked potatoes (okay if they are lumpy). In skillet, sauté SPAM® in a little oil; add onion, pepper, salt, sugar, and curry powder. Combine onion-SPAM™ mixture with potatoes. Add 1 egg and mix well. Form into patties. Roll in flour and then beaten eggs. Coat with panko or breadcrumbs. Heat oil in skillet and fry patties until golden brown.

Serve with curry-mayonnaise (mayonnaise mixed with curry powder to taste) on the side.

Frijole SPAM™ with Salsa

Serves 4

1 can SPAM® luncheon meat, cut into 8 slices (or Hot & Spicy SPAM®)
$1/_2$ cup flour
2 teaspoons chili powder
1 teaspoon oregano
$1/_2$ teaspoon pepper
$1/_4$ teaspoon cayenne pepper
$1/_2$ teaspoon garlic powder
vegetable oil for frying
$1/_2$ can refried beans
8 tablespoons salsa
1 cup grated cheese
lettuce, tomatoes, avocados, cilantro, and olives

Mix flour and seasonings. Heat vegetable oil in skillet. Dip SPAM® slices in flour and fry until golden brown. Place SPAM® in baking pan and top each slice with layer of refried beans and cheese. Bake in 350-degree oven until beans are heated and cheese is bubbly, about 10–15 minutes. Serve on bed of finely chopped lettuce. Top with salsa and garnish with tomatoes, avocados, cilantro, and olives.

Garlic Eggplant with SPAM®

Serves 4–6

1/4 cup soy sauce
1/2 cup water
2 tablespoons sugar
1 tablespoon vinegar
1 1/2 tablespoons cornstarch
1 tablespoon finely minced ginger
3 cloves garlic, minced
2 small red chili peppers or Tabasco® sauce to taste
4 long eggplants, sliced
2 tablespoons vegetable oil
1 can SPAM® luncheon meat, cut into logs

Combine soy sauce, water, sugar, vinegar, cornstarch, ginger, garlic, and chili peppers or Tabasco® sauce to taste in small bowl; set aside. Slice eggplant and place in bowl of cold water. Heat a little oil in large skillet and lightly brown SPAM®. Drain eggplant, put rest of oil in pan and cook eggplant with SPAM®. Before eggplant is completely done, add sauce and cook until eggplant is done and sauce is thickened, adding a bit more water if necessary. Serve with hot rice.

SPAM™ Hekka

Serves 4–6

2 tablespoons vegetable oil
1 can SPAM® luncheon meat, sliced
1 thin slice gingerroot, crushed
$1/2$ cup water
$1/2$ cup soy sauce
$1/3$ cup sugar
2 carrots, cut into matchstick slivers
1 (14-ounce) can bamboo shoots, sliced
1 cup sliced mushrooms
1 (14-ounce) block tofu, cubed
3 stalks green onion, sliced

Slice SPAM® into thin pieces, approximately 1 $1/2$ inches by $1/2$ inch. Heat oil in skillet and add gingerroot. Add SPAM® and cook 1 minute. Add water, soy sauce, and sugar. When sugar is dissolved, add carrots, bamboo shoots, mushrooms, and tofu. Cook about 2 minutes. Remove pan from stove and add green onion. Serve with hot rice.

Note: Locals call any sukiyaki-style dish "hekka." There are no set rules about which veggies to use. Use whatever you have on hand. Watercress, cabbage, or won bok are all good additions.

SPAM™-Stuffed Veggies

Serves 6–8

Veggies such as zucchini, eggplant, hasu (lotus root), and bell pepper
1 can SPAM® luncheon meat, ground or grated
dash of pepper
1 clove garlic, minced
1 stalk green onion, chopped
1 teaspoon toasted sesame seeds
1 egg, beaten
flour
2 eggs, beaten
vegetable oil for frying

Slice round veggies crosswise or on diagonal, about $1/4$ inch thick. If using bell peppers, slice them into sections. Combine SPAM®, pepper, garlic, green onion, sesame seeds, and 1 egg. Place spoonful of mixture on veggie slice, put another slice on top, and press together. Dip in flour, then beaten eggs, and fry in small amount of hot oil (nonstick skillet works well) over medium heat. Turn over and brown other side.

Dipping Sauce:
Combine
$1/2$ cup soy sauce
3 tablespoons rice vinegar
1–2 cloves garlic, minced
1 red chili pepper, thinly sliced (or chili pepper flakes)

Thai-Fry SPAM™ and Tofu

Serves 6

1 (14-ounce) block firm tofu
1 tablespoon curry powder
1 tablespoon grated ginger
1 tablespoon soy sauce
1 tablespoon fish sauce, such as nam pla
2 tablespoons vegetable oil
1 medium bok choy, sliced into 1-inch pieces
1 medium zucchini, halved and sliced
3 stalks green onion, sliced
1 medium red bell pepper, sliced
5 shiitake mushrooms, soaked in water
1 can SPAM® luncheon meat, cut into logs
1 $1/2$ teaspoons cornstarch
3 tablespoons water
$1/2$ cup fresh basil, chopped

Cut tofu into 1-inch cubes. In bowl large enough to hold tofu cubes, mix together curry powder, ginger, soy sauce, and fish sauce. In large nonstick skillet, heat some of oil and stir-fry bok choy, zucchini, green onion, and red bell pepper for 1–2 minutes. Remove to bowl. Drain mushrooms, reserving soaking liquid, and slice them into slivers. Remove tofu from curry mixture, reserving sauce. Heat a little oil in skillet and brown SPAM® and tofu. Add about $1/4$ cup of mushroom liquid to curry mixture and stir it into tofu-SPAM™. Bring to boil and add veggies and shiitake mushrooms. Mix cornstarch with water and stir into mixture. Add chopped basil and remove from heat. Serve with hot rice.

Note: Any combination of vegetables may be used. If you like a hot, spicy flavor, add a chopped red chili pepper or use Hot & Spicy SPAM® luncheon meat. For variety, a little coconut milk may be added at the end.

Japanese SPAM™ Loaf

Serves 4

1 (14-ounce) block firm tofu
1 can SPAM® luncheon meat, ground or grated (or Turkey SPAM®)
$1/_2$ envelope onion soup mix
2 eggs
2 stalks green onion, chopped
1 carrot, grated
$1/_2$ cup dry breadcrumbs

Sauce:
$1/_4$ cup soy sauce
3 tablespoons brown sugar
1 teaspoon grated ginger
1 clove garlic, minced
1 teaspoon prepared mustard

Place some paper towels on tofu and put heavy can or pan on it to drain excess water.

In large bowl, mash tofu, SPAM®, soup mix, eggs, green onion, carrot, and bread-crumbs. Form mixture into loaf and place in shallow pan. Bake for 20 minutes in 350-degree oven. Combine sauce ingredients in small pan and heat until sugar dissolves (you can also do this in microwave). Pour over loaf and bake 15 minutes.

SPAM™HEADS of the world: International Convention of Blockheads

SPAM™-Barley Soup

Serves 6

1 tablespoon vegetable oil
1 can SPAM® luncheon meat, cubed
2 cloves garlic, minced
1 small onion, chopped
2 (14-ounce) cans chicken broth
1 broth can water
1 (14-ounce) can diced tomatoes

1 tablespoon Worcestershire sauce
$1/2$ teaspoon pepper
$1/2$ cup pearl barley, rinsed
4 carrots, sliced
1 stalk celery, diced
1 zucchini, sliced
2 tablespoons fresh basil, chopped

In pot, heat oil and brown SPAM®. Add garlic and onion and cook until soft. Add broth, water, tomatoes (with juice), seasonings, and barley. Cook until barley is done, about 45 minutes. Add more water if soup is too thick. Add carrots, celery, and zucchini and cook until carrots are tender. Garnish with chopped basil.

Note: You may substitute other veggies, such as green beans, chopped cabbage, or other types of squash.

This soup is based on Beef/Barley Soup, a favorite dish from the Saari family's recipe collection.

Rice and Noodles

SPAM™ Fried Rice

Serves 3

1 ¹/₂ cups SPAM® luncheon meat
leftover rice, about 4 cups (cooked)
1 egg
1 tablespoon soy sauce
3 stalks green onion, chopped

Fry SPAM® in a bit of oil in skillet. Turn heat to low and add rice. Mix egg with soy sauce and add to rice and SPAM®. Add green onion just before serving.

  Note: Offer Tabasco® sauce.

Ramen Rice with SPAM®

Serves 4–6

1 can SPAM® luncheon meat, cubed
1 (3-ounce) package ramen noodles
4 cups cooked brown rice
1 tablespoon curry powder
$1/2$ cup raisins
1 cup chopped cilantro

good

In skillet, brown SPAM® cubes. Drain on paper towels. Break ramen noodles in package with bottom of pan or rolling pin. Mix crushed noodles with brown rice. Add curry powder and seasoning packet that comes with noodles (you may want to start with $1/2$ packet, taste, then add more as needed). Toss with SPAM® cubes, raisins, and chopped cilantro. Serve warm or cold.

"Now, Stevie, remember the two S-words: S-P-A-M™ and S-A-L-E."

Confetti Brown Rice

Serves 6

2 cups uncooked brown rice
1 tablespoon minced garlic
2 2/3 cups chicken broth
1 cup cooked black beans or gandule beans
1 can SPAM® luncheon meat, cubed (or Hot & Spicy SPAM®)
1/2 round onion, chopped

1 cup chopped red bell pepper
1/2 teaspoon cumin
dash of Tabasco® sauce
1/2 cup chopped cilantro
1/4 cup chopped mint
2 stalks green onion, chopped

Wash rice. Place in rice cooker with minced garlic and broth. Cook and let sit 15 minutes after rice cooker turns off. Rinse beans and drain well. Sauté SPAM® cubes in large skillet sprayed with vegetable oil spray. Add round onion and red pepper and cook until they are soft. Lower heat and add cooked rice and beans. Season with cumin and Tabasco® sauce. Remove from heat and add cilantro, mint, and green onion.

One of my personal favorites, this dish is reminiscent of gandule rice, but much easier to prepare. Canned gandule beans are available in Hispanic markets.

SPAM™ish Rice

Serves 4

2 tablespoons vegetable oil
1 can SPAM® luncheon meat, ground
1/2 small onion, minced
2 cloves garlic, minced
1/2 cup chopped green pepper
1 cup uncooked rice
1 (11-ounce) can tomato soup
1 soup can water
1 tablespoon Worcestershire sauce

Heat oil in skillet and cook SPAM®, onion, garlic, and green pepper until veggies are tender. Add all other ingredients, stir together, and bring to boil. Cover and cook over low heat, stirring occasionally, until rice is cooked (30–40 minutes).

Ramen-SPAM™ Salad

Serves 6

1 small head cabbage, finely shredded
2 stalks green onion, chopped
2 carrots, shredded
$1/2$ cup sliced radishes
1 can SPAM® luncheon meat, sliced and fried until almost crisp
1 (3-ounce) package ramen
1 cup unsalted peanuts, coarsely chopped
chopped cilantro (optional)

Dressing:
$1/2$ packet ramen seasoning
$1/3$ cup sugar
1 teaspoon pepper
$1/4$ teaspoon red pepper flakes
6 tablespoons rice wine vinegar
$1/2$ cup vegetable oil
1 tablespoon sesame oil

Shred and chop all vegetables and place in large bowl. Fry SPAM®, then cut into logs. Toss together with vegetables. Shake dressing ingredients together in jar. Crush ramen, using bottom of pan or rolling pin. Add to SPAM™-vegetable mixture and toss with dressing. Garnish with peanuts and cilantro.

Japanese Pasta Salad

Serves 6

1 can SPAM® luncheon meat
1 (16-ounce) package angel hair pasta, cooked
1 cucumber, cut into matchstick slivers
1 carrot, cut into matchstick slivers
1 stalk celery, thinly sliced
2 stalks green onion, chopped
Oriental-style salad dressing, to taste
1/2 jar furikake nori (seasoned nori flakes)

Fry **SPAM**® and cut into matchstick slivers. Boil pasta; drain well. In large bowl, toss together pasta, **SPAM**®, cucumber, carrot, celery, and green onion. Add dressing to taste. Chill well. Just before serving, sprinkle with nori.

Sesame Noodles and SPAM®

Serves 4

8 ounces udon noodles, boiled
4 tablespoons sesame oil
$1/_4$ cup chopped peanuts
1 can SPAM® luncheon meat, sliced
2 tablespoons chopped ginger
2 cloves garlic, minced
$1/_2$ red bell pepper, thinly sliced
1 cup snow peas
6 tablespoons teriyaki sauce (bottled)
2 tablespoons lemon juice
2 teaspoons chili-garlic hot sauce
2 stalks green onion, chopped

Boil noodles in water according to package directions; drain but do not rinse. Put noodles back in same pot and toss with 1 tablespoon of sesame oil and peanuts. In skillet, fry SPAM® slices until crispy. Drain on paper towels and cut into logs. In same skillet, heat remaining oil and stir-fry ginger, garlic, snow peas, and bell pepper. Mix together teriyaki sauce, lemon juice, and hot sauce and stir into noodles. Toss with stir-fried veggies and SPAM®. Garnish with chopped green onion.

Korean-Style Rice

Serves 4–6

hot cooked rice (about 8 cups)
1 package bean sprouts, blanched
1 bunch watercress, blanched
$1/_2$ can SPAM® luncheon meat, fried and cut into slivers (or Hot & Spicy SPAM®)
3 stalks green onion, chopped
1 tablespoon sesame oil
1 tablespoon soy sauce
2 cups kim chee, drained and chopped

Cook rice in your rice cooker. Blanch bean sprouts and watercress. Drain well and cut into 1-inch pieces. Fry SPAM® and drain on paper towels. Combine rice, SPAM®, veggies, sesame oil, soy sauce, and kim chee in large bowl.

Chinese-Style SPAM™ Paella

Serves 4

✓5 shiitake mushrooms, sliced
✓2 tablespoons oil
✓1 clove garlic, minced
1 tablespoon minced ginger
✓1 small onion, thinly sliced
1/3 cup sliced water chestnuts
✓1 can SPAM® luncheon meat, cut into bite-sized pieces
✓4 boneless chicken thighs, halved

✓1 1/2 cups chicken broth
✓3/4 cup uncooked rice
1 tablespoon hoi sin sauce
✓1 tablespoon soy sauce
✓1 teaspoon black beans, rinsed and mashed
✓1/2 pound shrimp, cleaned and shelled
✓black pepper, chili oil, and chopped cilantro

good

Soak shiitake mushrooms in water to soften; drain and slice. In large skillet heat oil and sauté garlic, ginger, and onion until tender. Add shiitake mushrooms and water chestnuts and cook 1 minute. Remove from pan. In same pan, brown SPAM® pieces. Remove SPAM® from pan and then brown chicken pieces. Add chicken broth, rice, onion mixture, and SPAM®. Bring to boil; season with hoi sin sauce, soy sauce, and black beans. Lower heat, cover pan, and cook for 20 minutes or until rice is done. Place raw shrimp on top of rice and cook 5 minutes or until shrimp is done. Stir in black pepper and chili oil to taste and garnish with chopped cilantro.

SPAM® and Long Rice

Serves 4

2 bundles long rice
1 tablespoon vegetable oil
2 teaspoons minced gingerroot
1 clove garlic, minced
$1/_2$ can SPAM® luncheon meat, cut into logs
1 tablespoon soy sauce
2 teaspoons oyster sauce
2 cups water
3 cups bean sprouts
3 stalks green onion, cut into 1-inch pieces

Soak long rice in warm water for 20 minutes; drain and cut into 3-inch pieces. Heat oil in large pan and cook ginger and garlic with SPAM® for 1 minute. Add seasonings and water and bring to boil. Put in long rice and cook 2–3 minutes. Add bean sprouts and green onion. Turn off heat. Stir and serve.

SPAM® 'n' Rice Casserole

Serves 4–6

1 can SPAM® luncheon meat, cubed
3 cups cooked rice (leftover)
2 stalks green onion, chopped
1 stalk celery, chopped
$1/2$ cup chopped water chestnuts
1 (11-ounce) can cream of mushroom soup
$1/3$ cup mayonnaise
1 tablespoon lemon juice
salt and pepper to taste

Combine all ingredients in bowl. Pour into casserole dish or 8x8-inch pan that has been sprayed with vegetable oil cooking spray. Bake for 40 minutes in 350-degree oven.

This is a quick and easy way to use leftover rice with staples that most locals have on hand.

Loco Moco SPAM®

Serves 4

1 tablespoon vegetable oil
1 clove garlic, minced
1 can SPAM® luncheon meat, grated
$1/2$ onion, chopped
1 (4-ounce) can mushroom pieces
1 tablespoon soy sauce

1 tablespoon oyster sauce
1 cup hot water
2 tablespoons cornstarch
4 tablespoons cold water
4 eggs
hot rice

Heat oil in large pan. Add garlic and grated SPAM® and sauté for 2–3 minutes. Add chopped onion and mushrooms. Add soy sauce and oyster sauce. Stir well and add hot water. Cook for 2 minutes. Mix cornstarch and cold water. Stir into pan and cook until sauce is thickened.

Using large spoon, make 4 depressions in SPAM™ mixture. Break an egg into each depression (you may want to cover pan at this point) and cook until eggs set. When eggs are done, scoop individual servings carefully onto plates of hot rice. Serve with Tabasco® sauce and ketchup and dig in.

This recipe is from Sandy Pak, who is originally from Hilo, home of the original Loco Moco.

SPAM™ Katsu Domburi

Serves 4–6

For Katsu:
1 can SPAM® luncheon meat, sliced
flour
2 eggs, beaten
panko (Japanese breadcrumbs)
vegetable oil for frying
hot rice

Dredge sliced SPAM® in flour, dip into eggs, coat with panko, and fry until golden brown. Set aside.

Sauce for rice:
1 cup water (add a little hondashi for added flavor)
2 teaspoons mirin
2 tablespoons soy sauce
4 teaspoons sugar
1 small Maui onion, thinly sliced
4 eggs
chopped green onion and nori for garnish

In frying pan, heat water, mirin, soy sauce, and sugar (adjust seasoning to your liking). Add onion and simmer until onion is soft. Add eggs, breaking them up. Place SPAM® luncheon meat on eggs. Fill domburi bowls with rice and scoop sauce over rice. Garnish with chopped green onions and shredded nori.

   Note: Hondashi is a Japanese seasoning; omit if unavailable. This dish is named for the serving bowl, domburi, a large rice bowl.

This recipe is from Lisa Apana of Maui.

SPAM™-Miso Udon

Serves 4

vegetable oil
$1/2$ can SPAM® luncheon meat, finely chopped
$1/2$ cup miso
1 tablespoon sugar
1 tablespoon sake
2 cups vegetable broth, chicken broth, or water
1 (10-ounce) package udon noodles, boiled
2 stalks green onion, chopped

Heat a little oil in skillet and brown SPAM®. Mix together miso, sugar, sake, and broth and cook 1–2 minutes with SPAM®. Prepare udon according to package directions. Drain, put in large bowl, and pour sauce over it. Garnish with chopped green onion.

Stir-Fry SPAM™ Spaghetti

Serves 4

1 can SPAM® luncheon meat, cut into logs
2 tablespoons olive oil
2 cloves garlic, minced
1 small onion, sliced
2 medium carrots, cut into matchstick slivers
1 cup snow peas
2 cups shredded cabbage
chopped cilantro for garnish
salt, pepper, red pepper flakes to taste
thin spaghetti (8–12 ounces)

Cook spaghetti according to package directions and drain. Heat oil in wok or large skillet and sauté garlic and onion. Add SPAM® logs and brown slightly. Add all veggies and cook until they are tender, but still crisp. Season with salt, pepper, and red pepper flakes. Add spaghetti and additional olive oil (to make spaghetti easier to handle). Adjust seasoning and garnish with chopped cilantro.

Breakfast and Brunch

The hammy quality of SPAM® luncheon meat lends itself to breakfast or brunch recipes. The standard local favorite is fried SPAM®, eggs, and rice, but here are some other ways to serve SPAM® for breakfast or brunch.

SPAM™ Addiction Egg and SPAM™ Napoleon Benedict

Serves 4

1 (7-ounce) package cornbread mix
1 can SPAM® luncheon meat, sliced
salsa (store kind is OK)
1 package Hollandaise sauce mix (fresh is better)
poached eggs (2 per serving)

Bake cornbread according to directions. Cool. Fry or grill SPAM® slices to your liking. (For each serving you will need 2 slices.) Prepare Hollandaise sauce according to package directions. Poach eggs (2 per serving).

To arrange, cut cornbread in shape of SPAM® luncheon meat. If bread is too thick, slice it in half. Layer cornbread, SPAM®, cornbread, SPAM®. Top Napoleon with 2 poached eggs, salsa, and Hollandaise sauce. Sprinkle with paprika.

This impressive creation was dreamed up by SPAM™ fan Kawika Paet of Bentos and Banquets, Wailuku, Maui.

Fruity Fritters

Serves 4–6

1 $1/_2$ cups flour
1 tablespoon sugar
$1/_2$ teaspoon salt
2 teaspoons baking powder
2 eggs, beaten
1 cup milk
1 tablespoon vegetable oil
$1/_2$ can SPAM® luncheon meat, diced (small)
1 $1/_2$ cups fruit, such as mangoes, apples, or peaches, chopped
$1/_3$ cup raisins
vegetable oil for frying
powdered sugar

Combine dry ingredients in bowl. Add eggs, milk, and oil; mix well. Add SPAM® and fruit. Heat about 1 inch of oil in skillet and drop spoonfuls of batter into it. Cook fritters until golden brown, turn over, and cook other side. Drain on paper towels and sprinkle with powdered sugar.

SPAM® and Rice Pancakes

Serves 4

$1/2$ can SPAM® luncheon meat, diced (small)
1 egg
2 tablespoons vegetable oil, plus additional for greasing pan
1 cup cooked rice (cold, leftover is best)
$3/4$ cup milk
1 tablespoon sugar
1 cup baking mix (Bisquick®)
cinnamon-sugar or syrup for topping

In large bowl, beat egg slightly. Add oil, rice, and milk. Add sugar and baking mix and combine well. Heat lightly greased griddle or large skillet. Pour about $1/4$ cup batter for each pancake (soup ladle works well). Cook on medium heat until bubbles appear and edges are dry; flip over and cook about $1\ 1/2$ minutes. Serve with butter and cinnamon-sugar or syrup. Makes a great breakfast with eggs!

Variation 1: To batter, add diced fruit such as mangoes, peaches, pears, or apples and dash of cinnamon.

Variation 2: Omit sugar from batter and add finely chopped green onion. Eat pancakes with sato-shoyu (sugar and soy sauce mixed together to taste) or hoi sin sauce.

SPAM® and Taro Oven Omelet

Serves 4–6

2 cups diced cooked taro
$1/2$ can SPAM® luncheon meat, diced
$1/2$ cup chopped water chestnuts
2 stalks green onion, chopped
1 teaspoon black pepper
1 tablespoon hoi sin sauce
1 tablespoon soy
5 eggs, beaten
$1/2$ cup water or broth
chopped cilantro for garnish

Cut taro in quarters, cover with water, and cook until it can be pierced with chopstick; do not overcook. Drain, peel and dice.

Mix together diced SPAM®, taro, water chestnuts, green onion, pepper, hoi sin sauce, and soy. Beat eggs and water or broth in bowl. Add SPAM™-taro mixture to eggs. Pour into greased 8x8-inch pan and bake at 350 degrees for about 20 minutes or until mixture is set. Cut into squares and garnish with chopped cilantro.

Plantation Delight

2 cups flour
$1/3$ cup sugar
1 tablespoon baking powder
2 eggs
1 $1/4$ cups milk
$1/2$ teaspoon vanilla or lemon extract
1 can SPAM® luncheon meat, sliced and fried
liliko'i butter or guava jelly

Mix together dry ingredients. Add eggs, milk, and vanilla or lemon extract. Grease small skillet (omelet pan) lightly with vegetable oil. Heat on stove. Pour half of batter in skillet, lower heat, and cook until bubbles appear on top. Flip pancake carefully (this is kind of scary at first; do it over sink). Continue cooking until pancake is done. Repeat with rest of batter. Cut each pancake into wedges. Spread with liliko'i butter or guava jelly and place piece of fried SPAM® luncheon meat in middle.

Note: This "marries" two plantation foods, SPAM® luncheon meat and plantation pancakes. Plantation workers had no ovens, but as some of the women went to work as maids at "haole house," they were exposed to cakes and started making these on the stove in cast iron skillets. Japanese called these "dango"— dumplings or cakes. I remember eating this treat as a child. With the help of David Hana'ike (of Super Macaroni and Cheese fame), I duplicated the pancakes after many trials. We found that a small cast iron skillet works best, but an omelet pan works also. There's no fat in the cakes, so don't feel bad about adding SPAM® luncheon meat!

93

Dilly SPAM™ Rolls

Serves 6

1 can SPAM® luncheon meat, chopped
1 tablespoon butter
2 cups fresh mushrooms, sliced
1 tablespoon minced garlic
$1/2$ cup finely chopped onion
1 stalk celery, finely chopped
$1/2$ cup slivered zucchini
1 teaspoon dill weed
$1/2$ cup Parmesan cheese
salt and pepper to taste
butter
bread dough (frozen or homemade)

Fry SPAM® until browned. Drain on paper towels. Sauté mushrooms and garlic in 1 tablespoon butter until limp. Season with salt and pepper. Add onion, celery, zucchini, and dill. Cook until veggies are limp. Add SPAM® and blend with veggies. Mix in Parmesan cheese; turn off heat and cool.

Prepare bread dough: If using frozen, thaw. Roll into 9x13-inch rectangle, about $1/2$-inch thick. Generously butter dough and spread with dilly SPAM™ mixture. Roll up dough

(lengthwise) like jellyroll as tightly as possible. Pinch ends to seal. Roll log in additional dill. Slice dough into 2-inch segments, place on cookie sheet, and let bread rise (about 30 minutes). Bake at 350 degrees until brown (about 25 minutes).

Shortcut: A favorite biscuit dough may be used in place of bread dough (no need to let dough rise).

This 'ono recipe comes from Debbie Yap of Ha'ikū, Maui.

SPAM™y Breakfast Cake

Serves 6–8

Topping:
3 tablespoons butter
$1/2$ can SPAM® luncheon meat, cut into $1/2$-inch cubes
1 almost ripe mango, peeled and cut into $1/2$-inch cubes
$1/2$ cup brown sugar
$1/2$ cup chopped macadamia nuts or pecans

Batter:
$3/4$ cup flour
2 $1/2$ teaspoons baking powder
$3/4$ cup cornmeal
$1/2$ cup sugar
$1/2$ teaspoon salt
$1/4$ cup vegetable oil
$3/4$ cup milk
1 egg, beaten
grated rind of one orange

Topping:
Melt butter in ovenproof skillet (cast iron works well) and cook SPAM® until lightly browned. Add mangoes and brown sugar and cook until sugar melts. Stir in nuts.

Batter:
In bowl, mix together dry ingredients. Add vegetable oil, milk, egg, and orange rind. Spread batter on top of mangoes and SPAM® luncheon meat. Bake at 375 degrees for about 25 minutes, or until golden and firm to touch.

Let cake stand in pan for 3 minutes, then run knife around edge. Invert cake onto plate, or cut into wedges and carefully place bottom-side-up on plates. Replace any of topping that is stuck to pan. Serve warm.

Note: Pineapple, apples, or peaches may be substituted for mangoes.

SPAM® and Potato Frittata

Serves 4

vegetable oil or spray
1 small onion, thinly sliced
$^1/_2$ can SPAM® luncheon meat, diced
1 small potato, cooked and diced
1 tablespoon minced green onion
5 eggs
pepper to taste
$^1/_2$ teaspoon oregano
$^1/_3$ cup grated cheese

Heat oil in 10-inch nonstick or cast iron skillet (ovenproof). Add onion slices and sauté about 2 minutes. Add SPAM® and brown lightly. Remove $^1/_2$ of this mixture and set aside. Add diced potato and green onion to skillet and mix with onion. Reduce heat to medium. With fork, beat eggs, pepper, and oregano and add to skillet. Do not stir. Cook just until bottom of eggs is set (3–4 minutes). Sprinkle reserved SPAM™-onion mixture on top. Place under broiler, about 4 inches away from heat, until eggs are set and top is golden. Sprinkle with grated cheese. Loosen edges and slide onto plate. Cut into wedges and garnish with sliced tomatoes.

"What? You got onion slicer, egg slicer, bagel slicer, cheese slicer, but no SPAM® slicer?"

SPAM™-Apple Quiche

Serves 6–8

1 can Smoke Flavored SPAM® luncheon meat
9-inch deep-dish pie crust (frozen)
1 cup shredded Cheddar cheese
1 cup shredded Monterey Jack cheese
2 large Granny Smith apples, peeled and thinly sliced
1 tablespoon sugar
$1/2$ teaspoon cinnamon
4 large eggs
1 cup half and half
1 tablespoon dry mustard
1 tablespoon Worcestershire sauce
$1/8$ teaspoon garlic salt

Slice SPAM® $1/4$-inch thick and fry slices until golden brown. (This will help reduce fat and provide a more desirable texture.) Cut SPAM® into cubes and reserve 1 cup for filling. Remainder can be used for garnish.

In oven preheated to 425 degrees, bake pie crust for 8 minutes. Remove from oven and spread half of two cheeses on bottom of pie crust. Place 1 cup SPAM® on top of cheeses. Spread apple slices evenly over cheese and SPAM® and sprinkle with sugar and cinnamon. Add remaining cheeses. Mix eggs and half-and-half together in blender. Add mustard, Worcestershire sauce, and garlic salt. Pour egg mixture into filled pie crust and bake in 350-degree oven for 45–55 minutes. Let this quiche cool for 10 minutes before slicing. Garnish with reserved SPAM® luncheon meat.

This recipe by Dave Mozdren won first place at the SPAMARAMA™ 2000 in Honolulu.

SPAM™ Quiche

1 9-inch deep-dish pie crust (frozen or your own)
1 cup broccoli, sliced
$1/2$ cup SPAM® luncheon meat, cut into $1/2$-inch strips
$1/4$ cup sliced onion
1 tablespoon butter
1 cup grated cheese (Swiss, Cheddar, or Jack)
3 eggs
1 (13-ounce) can evaporated milk
$1/4$ teaspoon nutmeg
$1/2$ teaspoon salt
dash of Tabasco® sauce
Parmesan cheese

Bake pie crust in 450-degree oven for 5 minutes. Set aside.

Parboil broccoli and drain. In small pan, sauté SPAM® and onion in butter until onion is limp. Fill crust with SPAM®, onion, broccoli, and grated cheese. In bowl beat together eggs, evaporated milk, nutmeg, salt, and Tabasco® sauce. Pour egg mixture over ingredients in pie crust. Sprinkle with Parmesan cheese. Bake at 425 degrees for 10 minutes. Reduce oven temperature to 350 degrees and bake 25–30 minutes or until quiche is set and golden brown. Cool 10 minutes before slicing.

Even haoles who say they don't eat SPAM® luncheon meat like this quiche.

Corny Quiche

Serves 6

$1/2$ can SPAM® luncheon meat, sliced (or Smoke Flavored)
3 eggs
$1/4$ teaspoon salt
$1/2$ small onion, chopped
1 (13-ounce) can evaporated milk
3 tablespoons butter, melted
2 cups fresh corn kernels (or frozen)
1 9-inch deep-dish pie crust (frozen or your own)

Fry SPAM® slices until crispy; drain on paper towels. Cut into 1-inch pieces.

Combine eggs, salt, and onion in blender and blend until onion is finely chopped. Add evaporated milk and butter and blend. If using fresh corn, cut kernels off cob. Place corn in bowl and mix in milk and eggs. Bake crust in pre-heated 425-degree oven for 8 minutes. Put SPAM® slices in crust and pour egg-corn mixture over them. Reduce oven temperature to 375 degrees and bake for about 45 minutes or until set. Cool slightly before cutting.

Note: This can be a crustless quiche. Omit pie crust and pour into buttered pie pan.

Smoked SPAM™ Brunch Casserole

Serves 6–8

2 cups broccoli florets (small pieces)
4 stalks green onion, chopped
1 can Smoke Flavored SPAM® luncheon meat, sliced thinly (crosswise)
2 cups grated Monterey Jack cheese
1 (8-ounce) package cream cheese, cut into small cubes
8 eggs
2 cups milk (not nonfat)
1 cup baking mix (Bisquick®)
dash of salt
$1/2$ teaspoon pepper

Spray 9x13-inch pan with vegetable oil cooking spray. Arrange broccoli and half of green onions over bottom of pan. Cover with SPAM®, cheese, cream cheese, and rest of green onion. Mix together eggs, milk, baking mix, salt and pepper in blender and pour over SPAM™ and cheese mixture. Bake in 375-degree oven for about 30 minutes. Cool 10 minutes before slicing.

Breakfast Bread Pudding

Serves 6

5 cups bread cubes
$1/_2$ can SPAM® luncheon meat, cubed
1 apple, peeled and diced
$1/_2$ cup raisins
2 $1/_2$ cups milk
$1/_4$ cup melted butter (optional)
$3/_4$ cup brown sugar
3 eggs
1 teaspoon cinnamon
1 teaspoon vanilla

Spray an 8x8-inch pan with vegetable oil cooking spray. Place bread cubes, SPAM®, apple, and raisins in pan and mix together. Mix all other ingredients together and pour over bread. Allow bread to absorb milk-egg mixture for a few minutes; then bake in 350-degree oven for 45 minutes. Cool 10 minutes before serving.

Quick and Easy

One of the reasons SPAM® luncheon meat has retained its popularity over the years is that it is so adaptable and so compatible with other convenience products. With a can of SPAM® and cans, bottles, jars, and packages of everyday pantry items, you can concoct an edible fast meal. These dishes are convenient when you are under stress and strapped for time, or perhaps in situations such as camping or waiting out a hurricane, when you must rely on canned, bottled, or dry items. Living on islands, people in Hawaiʻi have an "always be prepared" mindset, a stockpile mentality that mainlanders have difficulty comprehending. But with a can of SPAM® and some other staples from the pantry, you won't starve. Don't knock it until you've tried it—these recipes are quite ʻono!

Local Staples

SPAM™ Katsu

Serves 4

Katsu is derived from the popular Japanese dish tonkatsu, which literally means "pork cutlet." Dipped in egg and panko (Japanese breadcrumbs), tonkatsu is the Japanese version of wienerschnitzel. In addition to tonkatsu, we also eat chicken katsu. When you don't have fresh pork or chicken, try this SPAM™ version.

flour
1 can SPAM® luncheon meat, sliced into 8 pieces
2 egg whites, beaten with fork until frothy
panko or fine breadcrumbs
vegetable oil for frying

Put a little flour on piece of waxed paper or foil. Coat SPAM® with flour, dip in beaten egg whites, and coat with panko. Heat some oil in skillet and fry SPAM® until golden brown. Drain on paper towels and serve with sauce.

110

Sauce:
$1/2$ cup ketchup
$1/4$ teaspoon pepper
2–3 tablespoons Worcestershire sauce
Tabasco® sauce to taste

Variation: Curry SPAM™ Katsu

Make SPAM™ katsu and slice into bite-sized pieces. Make some prepared curry sauce, such as S & B brand, adding veggies if desired. Put SPAM™ katsu on mound of hot rice and pour curry sauce over it.

Kakimochi-Furikake SPAM™ Katsu

Cut **SPAM®** luncheon meat into 16 pieces (make 8 lengthwise slices and then cut those slices in half crosswise). Follow directions for **SPAM™** Katsu (page 110), substituting kakimochi (Japanese rice crackers) and furikake (dried nori flakes) for panko. To crush kakimochi, place between two sheets of waxed paper or in plastic bag and pound with can (or use rolling pin). You can also grind in blender. Mix crushed kakimochi with furikake and follow steps for **SPAM™** Katsu.

This makes a good fast pūpū.

Camper's Saucy SPAM®

Serves 2

1 can SPAM® luncheon meat
barbecue sauce

Fry slices of SPAM®. Add some prepared barbecue sauce (any brand will do) and simmer for a few minutes. Serve over hot rice or in rolls.

This recipe is from camper of the Northwest Territory Charleen Ego.

SPAMBURGER™ Steak

Serves 3

Grind SPAM® luncheon meat to coarse texture with meat grinder or food processor and add chopped onion. Press into patties and fry. Serve with packaged brown gravy mix and hot rice.

Contributed by Robert G. (Bobby) Hill III

Seared SPAM® with Hawaiian Slaw

Serves 3–4

1 can SPAM® luncheon meat, sliced (or Hot & Spicy SPAM®)
head cabbage
mayonnaise
soy sauce

Cook SPAM® slices in very hot cast iron skillet or any old pan to give it a nice crispy brown crust.

Hawaiian Slaw:
Chop some cabbage very finely. Mix mayo and soy together to taste. Some people like plenty mayo. Adjust to your taste. Toss dressing with cabbage. Mound on plate and top with SPAM® slices. Serve with hot rice.

Note: There is a Japanese contraption available at Asian kitchen supply stores that looks and works like a large vegetable peeler and makes really fine slaw.

Korean-Style SPAM®

Serves 4

1 can SPAM® luncheon meat, cut into logs
1 (12-ounce) jar kim chee
1 small onion, sliced
2 teaspoons soy sauce

Brown SPAM® logs in skillet. Place kim chee in strainer or colander and rinse with water (if you like it hot, do not rinse). Drain well. Add kim chee, onion, and soy sauce to SPAM® and cook 2 minutes.

Lloyd Pak, who gave me this recipe, says this dish is also good with sliced zucchini and tofu added.

Beach Soup

Serves 6

2 cans SPAM® luncheon meat, cubed
1 round onion, chopped
2 (8-ounce) cans tomato sauce
2 (15-ounce) cans kidney beans
1 carrot
2 potatoes, cubed (optional)
Hawaiian salt to taste
about 3 kidney bean cans of water, or water to cover

In pot, fry SPAM® and onion until brown. Add tomato sauce, beans, and water to cover. Add vegetables and salt. Bring to boil and simmer until vegetables are tender. Serve with hot rice or poi.

SOUPDAY!

Beach Soup is based on a dish that Lea Medeiros fondly remembers from her childhood. Her Uncle Manuel Paiva of Papakōlea used to cook it after taking her and other kids to Sandy Beach in his Ford Fairlane. While the food is simple, it evokes for her happy memories of beach days and a very special uncle. For many local people, like Lea, SPAM® luncheon meat brings back warm feelings of friends, family, good times, and happy days.

"Well, do I get SPAM® for lunch?"

SPAM is a registered trademark of Hormel Foods, LLC for luncheon meat.

SPAM® 'n' Takuwan

(Pickled Daikon)

Serves 4

takuwan, 6–7 inches long, or 1 jar sliced takuwan
1 teaspoon vegetable oil
$1/2$ can SPAM® luncheon meat, cut into logs
2 teaspoons soy sauce
1 teaspoon sugar
1 teaspoon sesame oil
sesame seeds

If using takuwan from a jar, drain. If using long takuwan, cut into thin slices. Soak takuwan slices in cold water for 20 minutes. In skillet, heat oil and sauté SPAM®. Drain takuwan and add to SPAM®. Season with soy sauce, sugar, and sesame oil and remove from heat. Sprinkle with sesame seeds.

This is good picnic food. Excellent with plain musubi.

SPAM™-Egg Ramen

Serves 2–3

2 (3-ounce) packages ramen noodles
4 eggs
1 tablespoon vegetable oil
$^1/_2$ can SPAM® luncheon meat, diced
chopped green onion for garnish

Cook ramen according to directions and drain. (Set aside flavor packets.) In large bowl mix eggs and one of flavor packets with fork. Add boiled noodles. Heat oil in large skillet (nonstick works well), add egg-noodle mixture, and sprinkle SPAM® on top. Lower heat to medium and brown egg-noodle mixture. Flip over and brown other side. Flip onto plate and sprinkle with green onion. Cut into wedges.

Scrambled Tofu and SPAM®

Serves 4

2 tablespoons vegetable oil
$1/2$ block tofu
$1/2$ small onion, minced
$1/2$ can SPAM® luncheon meat, diced
6 eggs
1 tablespoon soy sauce
chopped green onion for garnish

In large skillet heat oil (nonstick skillet works well). Put tofu in pan and break it up with spatula and cook over medium heat until moisture evaporates. Add onion and SPAM®. Beat eggs and soy sauce lightly with fork, mix into tofu mixture, and cook until eggs are set.

Serve on bed of chopped watercress with hot rice on the side. Offer Tabasco® sauce, ketchup, and furikake nori.

Super Macaroni and Cheese

Serves 3–4

1 (7-ounce) box macaroni and cheese dinner
3 tablespoons butter
2 cloves garlic, minced
1 cup sliced mushrooms (canned okay)
$1/2$ can SPAM® luncheon meat, cubed
grated Cheddar cheese, optional

Prepare macaroni and cheese according to directions on box. Melt butter in skillet. Add garlic, mushrooms, and cubed SPAM® and cook until mushrooms are soft (if using fresh ones). Add mushrooms and SPAM® to prepared macaroni and cheese. Place in casserole dish and sprinkle top with additional grated cheese if desired. Bake for 25–30 minutes in 350-degree oven.

Little kids love this dish, which was contributed by David Hana'ike.

Amanda's Squash 'n' SPAM®

Serves 4

1 tablespoon vegetable oil
2 cloves garlic, minced
1 handful dry shrimp
2 cans SPAM® luncheon meat, sliced into bite-sized pieces
1 medium squash, such as tongan, cubed
black pepper to taste
1 packet Sweet'N Low® (or sugar)
oyster sauce to taste

Heat oil in pot. Fry garlic, shrimp, and SPAM® until SPAM® is lightly browned. Add squash and cook until tender. Season with pepper, sugar, and oyster sauce.

Note: "Tongan" is a large squash frequently used in Asian dishes. It is also called "winter melon." You may substitute any white-fleshed squash, such as zucchini or chayote.

This easy recipe is from Amanda Martin of Wailuku, Maui.

Cook-Do SPAM™ Tofu

Serves 4

1 teaspoon vegetable oil
$3/4$ can SPAM® luncheon meat, grated or finely chopped
1 (14-ounce) block firm tofu
1 box Cook-Do seasoning sauce
2 stalks green onion, chopped

Fry grated SPAM® in oil. Cut tofu into $3/4$-inch cubes. Add Cook-Do seasoning sauce to SPAM®. Add tofu and carefully toss. Add chopped green onions and remove from heat. Eat with hot rice.

Cook-Do seasoning is available in the Asian section of most markets.

Sanchu SPAM™
(Korean SPAM™ Rolls)

Leaf lettuce, washed and dried
hot rice
SPAM® luncheon meat, sliced, fried, and cut into logs
kochu jang sauce
kim chee

Place all items on table. Put rice on lettuce leaf, spread kochu jang on rice, put SPAM® and kim chee on top, roll up, and enjoy!

SPAM®, String Beans, and Eggs

Serves 4

1 tablespoon oil
$^1/_2$ can SPAM® luncheon meat, cut into matchstick slivers
1 (8-ounce) package string beans, thinly sliced
3–4 eggs
salt and pepper to taste

Put oil in skillet and stir-fry SPAM® and string beans. Do not overcook beans. Break eggs into small bowl and beat with fork. Pour eggs over SPAM® and beans and cook until eggs are set. Add salt and pepper to taste.

SPAM™y-Corn Scallop

Serves 4–6

2 cans SPAM® luncheon meat, cubed (or Turkey SPAM®)
1 (14-ounce) can cream-style corn
1 (14-ounce) can corn niblets
$1/2$ small onion, minced
1 (11-ounce) can cream of mushroom soup
$1/2$ cup milk
black pepper to taste

Place cubed SPAM® in pot. Add all other ingredients and heat until bubbly. Add more milk if necessary. Serve on hot rice.

Note: This easy recipe is based on a favorite Honolulu school cafeteria lunch, turkey-corn scallop (leftover turkey and gravy with corn). SPAM®, canned corn, and cream of mushroom soup are staples in any Hawaiian pantry.

Pita Pocket SPAM™

Serves 6

3 cups grated potatoes (or use frozen hash browns)
1 tablespoon vegetable oil
1 can SPAM® luncheon meat, coarsely chopped
$1/2$ head cabbage (small), chopped
1 carrot, sliced
$1/2$ teaspoon pepper
2 tablespoons soy sauce
1 package (6) pita bread

Coarsely grate potatoes. Heat oil in large skillet and sauté potatoes until they are almost done. Add SPAM®, cabbage, carrot, and seasonings and cook until cabbage is done but still crunchy. Split pita bread and stuff with filling.

Miscellaneous Munchies

Hawaiian Hoagy

(In honor of Hoagy Gamble, SPAM™ distributor, Honolulu)

Hoagie rolls (or any kind of sandwich rolls)
SPAM® luncheon meat, sliced and fried or straight from can (or Turkey SPAM®)
canned corned beef, thinly sliced
Maui onions, thinly sliced
Swiss or Provolone cheese, sliced
cucumbers, thinly sliced
tomatoes, thinly sliced
lettuce, finely shredded
cilantro, chopped
kim chee, drained and chopped (optional)
Dressing: mayo mixed with a little soy sauce (not too much) and some wasabi paste

Split rolls and spread with dressing (if you prefer, can mix dressing with lettuce so it resembles coleslaw). Layer ingredients and enjoy.

Note: If you chill the corned beef before slicing, you can pick off the fat easily with the tip of a knife. Sliced Vienna sausage may also be added.

Hoagy tells me no worry: "The can keeps all that wonderful pork sealed up nice and tight and deflects bad luck!" (Note to mainlanders: People in Hawai'i believe it's bad luck to carry pork over the Pali.)

SPAM is a registered trademark of Hormel Foods, LLC for luncheon meat.

Sweet Potato–SPAM™ Mochi

Serves 12

1 (16-ounce) box mochiko (rice flour)
1 teaspoon baking soda
pinch of salt
1 cup brown sugar
1 (13-ounce) can coconut milk
1 $1/_4$ cups water
2 cups cooked and diced sweet potatoes (regular or Okinawan)
$1/_2$ can SPAM® luncheon meat, diced
1 tablespoon sesame seeds
kinako (soybean flour)

Spray 9x13-inch pan with cooking spray. In large bowl, mix mochiko, baking soda, salt, and brown sugar. Add coconut milk and water. Fold in cooked sweet potatoes and SPAM®. Pour into pan, sprinkle with sesame seeds, and cover pan with foil. Bake in 350-degree oven for 45 minutes. Remove foil and continue baking for 15 minutes or until done. Cool, cut into pieces, and roll in kinako.

SPAM™ochi Surprise

Serves 10

2 cups mochiko (rice flour)
1 1/2 cups sugar
2 cups water
food coloring (optional)
SPAM® luncheon meat, sliced
vegetable oil

Mix mochiko, sugar, and water together until smooth. If desired, tint batter SPAM® color using red and yellow food coloring. Spray microwave Bundt pan with vegetable oil spray and pour batter into it. Cover with plastic wrap and cook for about 12 minutes on high, rotating pan twice if your microwave does not revolve. You may have to adjust cooking time according to your microwave. Mochi should be firm to touch.

When mochi is cool, slice into thin pieces. Form mochi into SPAM® shape with your fingers. Slice SPAM® crosswise and sandwich a slice between 2 pieces of mochi, pinching edges to seal. Heat a little oil in nonstick skillet and brown mochi on both sides. Serve warm with sato-shoyu dipping sauce.

Sato-shoyu sauce: Put some white sugar in small dish and add soy sauce to taste.

Furikake-Mochi SPAM™

Serves 12

butter or vegetable oil
12 small prepared mochi
$1/2$ can SPAM® luncheon meat, finely chopped
furikake nori
finely chopped green onion
sato-shoyu

**Heat a little butter or oil in nonstick skillet
and lightly brown mochi. Sprinkle with
chopped SPAM®, furikake nori, and green
onion. Serve with sato-shoyu dipping
sauce. (See previous recipe.)**

Note: If you like your SPAM® crispy, fry it before putting on top of mochi.

Bev Hashimoto contributed this recipe.

136

Taro–Sweet Potato–SPAM™ Bake

Serves 6

1 1/2 pounds taro, cooked and sliced
1 1/2 pounds sweet potatoes, cooked and sliced
1 can SPAM® luncheon meat, sliced crosswise
1/2 cup raisins
1/2 cup butter, melted
1/3 cup brown sugar
1 cup coconut milk
1/2 cup chopped macadamia nuts

Steam or boil taro and sweet potatoes separately. Grease casserole dish and layer taro, sweet potatoes, SPAM®, and raisins. Combine melted butter, brown sugar, and coconut milk and pour over SPAM®, taro, and potatoes. Bake at 350 degrees for 40 minutes. Garnish with chopped nuts.

"You said you wanted to try our regional specialty.
It's blackened SPAM® luncheon meat with mayo-soy sauce and rice!"

Kim Chee Soup

Serves 6

1 (12-ounce) jar kim chee
1 tablespoon vegetable oil
1 can SPAM® luncheon meat, cut into logs
1 clove garlic, minced
2 (14-ounce) cans vegetable broth
2 broth cans water (more if desired)
1 zucchini, sliced
$1/_2$ block tofu, cubed
2 stalks green onion, chopped

Drain kim chee, reserving liquid. Rinse kim chee if you want a milder flavor. In pot, heat oil and stir-fry SPAM®, kim chee, and garlic. Add kim chee juice, broth, and water. Taste; add more water if necessary. Add zucchini and bring to boil. Lower heat and add tofu and green onion.

SPAM™-Potato Lumpia

Serves 12

$^1/_2$ can SPAM® luncheon meat
3 Okinawan sweet potatoes, parboiled
12 lumpia wrappers
vegetable oil for frying
$^1/_2$ cup honey

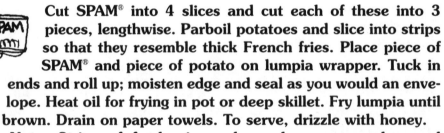

Cut SPAM® into 4 slices and cut each of these into 3 pieces, lengthwise. Parboil potatoes and slice into strips so that they resemble thick French fries. Place piece of SPAM® and piece of potato on lumpia wrapper. Tuck in ends and roll up; moisten edge and seal as you would an envelope. Heat oil for frying in pot or deep skillet. Fry lumpia until brown. Drain on paper towels. To serve, drizzle with honey.
Note: Strips of fresh pineapple or banana may be used instead of potatoes.

140

Taro Cake

Serves 10

4 cups cooked taro, cubed (small)
1 can SPAM® luncheon meat, finely chopped
4 shiitake mushrooms
1 cup mochiko (rice flour)
1 cup cornstarch

1 cup water
6 water chestnuts, chopped
2 tablespoons sliced Chinese salted olives
1 tablespoon soy sauce
1 tablespoon oyster sauce

Cut taro into large chunks and cook in water until it can be pierced with fork or chopstick. Peel and cut into small cubes. Soak shiitake mushrooms in warm water. When soft, squeeze out water and chop.

In large bowl, mix mochiko, cornstarch, and 1 cup water. Use wooden spoon or rice paddle to mix it. If mixture seems too thick, add more water. Add taro, SPAM®, chopped mushrooms, water chestnuts, olives, and seasonings. Grease 2 8-inch cake pans and divide taro mixture evenly in pans. Cover with foil and steam for 30 minutes. Cool and cut into wedges.

Note: Chinese salted olives are available in jars at Asian grocery stores. If unavailable substitute Kalamata olives.

141

Spicy SPAM™-Apple Pie

Serves 6

3 apples, peeled and diced
2 tablespoons lemon juice
1 teaspoon cinnamon
$^1/_2$ teaspoon nutmeg
$^1/_2$ teaspoon allspice
1 tablespoon flour
$^1/_3$ cup raisins
3 tablespoons sugar (optional)
$^1/_2$ can SPAM® luncheon meat, diced
1 9-inch deep-dish pie crust (frozen)

Topping:
$^1/_2$ cup flour
$^1/_2$ cup oatmeal
$^1/_2$ cup brown sugar
1 teaspoon cinnamon
2 tablespoons butter
1 tablespoon vegetable oil

Mix together apples and lemon juice. Add spices, flour, raisins, sugar, and SPAM®. Pour into crust. In small bowl, mix together topping ingredients. Sprinkle on top of pie filling and bake in 425-degree oven 10 minutes. Lower heat to 350 degrees and bake about 45–50 minutes or until apples are soft when poked with knife. Serve warm.

Why a SPAM™ pie? Why not? I just wanted to include a SPAM™ dessert. Besides, it is a conversation piece. Try serving it at your next local get-together.

Sweet Potato Salad

Serves 4

3–4 Okinawan sweet potatoes, cooked and cubed
1/2 can SPAM® luncheon meat, cubed
1 cucumber, sliced
1/2 Maui onion, thinly sliced
1 cup broccoli florets

Dressing:
1/4 cup vegetable oil
3 tablespoons sesame oil
1/2 cup soy sauce
1 tablespoon sugar
juice of 1/2 lemon

Place all ingredients in large bowl. Just before serving, add dressing and toss.

Note: Cooked taro or yellow sweet potatoes may be substituted for Okinawan potatoes, or a combination of potatoes may be used. This is a colorful dish.

Hawaiian Okazu-ya–Style
Macaroni and SPAM™ Salad

Serves 6

Many transplanted locals have told me that one of the foods they get 'ono for (crave) is Hawaiian-style macaroni salad as made by okazu-ya (Japanese delis). In this kind of macaroni salad, the macaroni is "fat"—that is, well done. The trick is to cook it well, but not to the point of falling apart. Unlike traditional haole-style macaroni salad, few ingredients go into this one. But you must use Best Foods Mayonnaise®! Adding cubes of SPAM® to this dish brings together two of our local favorites.

1 package elbow macaroni
1 carrot, grated
salt and pepper to taste
3/4 teaspoon sugar
Best Foods Mayonnaise® thinned with a little milk
  (3–4 tablespoons to 1 cup of mayo)
1 can SPAM® luncheon meat, cubed

In large pot of salted water, cook macaroni until it is plump. Watch it carefully. Drain in colander. In large bowl, gently mix together remaining ingredients with cooked macaroni. Start with 1 cup of mayo, adding more mayo if necessary. Chill before serving.

Glossary

Aburage: Fried tofu

Bittermelon: Spiny green vegetable with slight bitter taste

Cilantro: Herb of the parsley family, also called "Chinese parsley" or "coriander"

Domburi: Rice dish with sauce served in a deep bowl that is also called "domburi"

Empanada: Turnover with meat, fruit, or vegetable filling

Fishcake: Paste made by scraping the flesh of certain fish; also called " 'ō'io" or "surimi"

Furikake nori: Seasoned flaked seaweed used to season rice

Gandule: Small beans used in Hispanic dishes; also called "pigeon peas"

Frijole (Spanish): Beans

Hasu: Lotus root

Hekka: Local name for dish of meat and vegetables cooked in soy sauce

Hondashi: Japanese flavor-enhancer

Kakimochi: Japanese seasoned rice crackers

Kal-bi: Korean-style short ribs

Katsu: Breaded cutlet

Kim chee: Korean pickled vegetables with spicy seasonings

Kinako: Soybean flour, often used to coat mochi pieces

Kochu jang: Korean hot sauce

Loco moco: Local fast food consisting of hamburger patty on rice topped with fried eggs and gravy

Long rice: Dry, transparent noodles made out of mung bean starch

Lumpia: Fried Filipino vegetable/meat roll

Miso: Fermented soybean paste

Mochi: Japanese rice cake made of rice flour
Mochiko: Rice flour
Mun doo: Korean dumplings filled with vegetables and meat
Musubi: Rice ball
Nori: Seaweed in various forms. Nori sheets are used to roll sushi and musubi.
Okazu-ya: Japanese deli
Okinawan potato: A sweet potato with purple flesh
Oyster sauce: Chinese seasoning made out of fermented oysters
Panko: Japanese-style breadcrumbs
Papakōlea: Hawaiian homestead community in Honolulu
Pinacbet: Filipino vegetable stew with bits of meat
Pūpū: Appetizer
Ramen: Popular Japanese noodles sold dry in small packages
Sato-shoyu: Sugar–soy sauce mixture used as seasoning or dipping sauce
Shiitake: Japanese mushrooms
Somen: Thin Japanese wheat noodles
Taro: Starchy tuber used to make poi and other dishes in Hawai'i
Tofu: Soybean curd
Udon: Thick Japanese wheat noodles
Ume: Pickled plum
Wasabi: Japanese horseradish
Water chestnut: Small, crunchy tuber used in Asian cookery
Won ton: Chinese dumpling filled with meat